The Amazing Book of SPACE

ARCTURUS

This edition published in 2019 by Arcturus Publishing Limited
26/27 Bickels Yard, 151–153 Bermondsey Street,
London SE1 3HA

Author: Giles Sparrow
Editors: Joe Harris, Clare Hibbert, and Samantha Hilton
Designer: Amy McSimpson and Trudi Webb

ISBN: 978-1-78950-838-3
CH007562NT
Supplier 29, Date 0719, Print run 9203

Printed in China

The Amazing Book of SPACE

CONTENTS

Introduction

Our Universe is a huge area of space made up of everything we can see in every direction. It contains a great number of different objects—from tiny specks of cosmic dust to mighty galaxy superclusters. The most interesting of these are planets, stars and nebulae, galaxies, and clusters of galaxies.

Stars

A star is a dense (tightly packed) ball of gas that shines through chemical reactions in its core (middle). Our Sun is a star. Stars range from red dwarfs much smaller and fainter than the Sun, to supergiants a hundred times larger and a million times brighter.

Planets

A planet is a large ball of rock or gas that orbits (travels around) a star. In our solar system there are eight "major" planets, several dwarf planets, and countless smaller objects. These range from asteroids and comets down to tiny specks of dust.

Nebulae

The space b
stars is filled
unseen clou
dust called n
they collapse
grow dense
form new st
up from wit

Galaxies

A galaxy is a huge cloud of stars, gas, and dust, including nebulae, held together by a force called gravity. There are many different types of galaxy. This is because their shape, the nature of their stars, and the amount of gas and dust within them can vary.

This is our home galaxy, the Milky Way, seen from Earth. Our view of the Universe depends on what we can see using the best technologies that we have.

Galaxy Clusters

Gravity makes galaxies bunch together to form clusters that are millions of light-years wide. These clusters join together at the edges to form even bigger superclusters—the largest structures in the Universe.

The Solar System

The solar system is the region of space that surrounds our star, the Sun. It holds billions of objects, from tiny pieces of dust and icy boulders to eight major planets, some of them far larger than Earth.

Eight Planets and More

The planets of the solar system are split into two main groups. Close to the Sun there are four fairly small rocky planets. Earth is the third of these in order from the Sun, and also the largest. Farther out, past a region made up of shards and chunks of rock, there are four much larger worlds: the gas and ice giant planets.

Mars is the outermost of the rocky planets. It is just over half the size of Earth.

Venus, the second planet, is almost the same size as Earth.

The solar system formed from gas and dust left orbiting the newborn Sun about 4.5 billion years ago.

Mercury is the smallest planet and the closest to the Sun.

Earth is the only rocky planet with a large natural satellite, the Moon.

SOLAR SYSTEM PROFILE

Planets: Eight
Radius of orbit of most distant planet, Neptune:
4.5 billion km (2.8 billion miles)
Radius of heliosphere:
18 billion km (11.2 billion miles)
Region ruled by Sun's gravity:
Four light–years across

Where Does It End?

Astronomers haven't agreed on where exactly the solar system comes to an end. Some say it only reaches a little way past the orbits of the planets, just as far as the heliosphere—the region that the solar wind (particles streaming out from the Sun) covers. Others say it reaches as far as the Sun's gravity can hold onto objects: about halfway to the nearest star.

Jupiter is the fifth planet, and by far the largest.

Space probes have discovered changes in the solar wind as they leave the heliosphere.

Neptune, the farthest planet from the Sun, is nearly four times bigger than Earth.

Uranus is an ice giant, quite a bit smaller than Jupiter or Saturn.

Saturn was the most distant planet known in ancient times.

Saturn is famous for its rings. However, all the giant planets have ring systems—they are just a lot fainter.

The Sun

Our Sun is a fairly average, middle-aged star. It doesn't stand out, compared to other stars we know, but the heat, light, and streams of particles it pours out across the solar system set the conditions on Earth and all the other planets.

Solar Features

The Sun's surface is made up of extremely hot gas, with a temperature of around 5,500 °C (9,900 °F). Hot gas from inside the Sun rises to the surface, cools down by releasing light, and then sinks back toward the core. A non-stop stream of particles is also released from the surface, forming a solar wind that blows across the solar system.

Earth's magnetic field shields it from passing solar wind.

The Solar Cycle

Some features on the Sun come and go over time. Dark areas called sunspots form and then disappear, and so do huge loops of gas, called prominences, that rise high above the Sun. Most impressive of all are outbursts called solar flares, which release huge amounts of radiation (energy) and hot gas. All this activity repeats itself every 11 years because of changes in the Sun's magnetic field.

Never look directly at the Sun—it's so bright that you risk damaging your eyes. Astronomers study it with special telescopes.

Prominences are created when gas flows along loops of magnetic field that stick out of the Sun's surface. There is usually a sunspot group at each end.

SUN PROFILE

SUN

Diameter: 1.39 million km (864,000 miles)
Distance: 149.6 million km (93 million miles)
Rotation period: Approx 25 days
Mass: 333,000 x Earth

The surface of the Sun that can be seen is called the photosphere. It marks a region where the Sun's gas becomes transparent.

Dark sunspots are much cooler than their surroundings, with temperatures of about 3,500 °C (6,300 °F).

Mercury and Ven

Two scorching-hot rocky planets orbit closer to the Sun than Earth. Venus is almost the same size to Earth but with a very different atmosphere. Mercury is a tiny world much like our Moon, which speeds around the Sun in just 88 days.

Roasted Surfaces

Temperatures on both Mercury and Venus reach more than 430 °C (800 °F), but Venus is actually hotter than Mercury although it is farther from the Sun. That is because Venus's atmosphere traps heat. This means that the temperature is about 460 °C (860 °F) both day and night. Mercury has no atmosphere, so temperatures on its night side can drop to -170 °C (-280 °F).

Mercury's surface has many craters (holes), like our Moon. This picture has been treated to reveal surface features.

3D view of a Venusian volcano called Maat Mons

Venus has a thick, toxic atmosphere that isn't shown in this picture, so that we can see the surface beneath.

This view of Venus uses radar maps from the *Magellan* space probe.

Venus's landscape features volcanoes and cooled, solid lava.

VENUS PROFILE

VENUS

Diameter: 12,104 km (7,522 miles)
Length of day: 243 Earth days
Length of year: 225 Earth days
Number of moons: None

Our

Earth is the largest of
also the one with th
home world mostly
changing through a

World of Water

Earth's orbit around th
region astronomers ca
zone. The temperature
the surface is not too h
cold, but "just right" f
water. A "water cycle"
this life-giving chemic
between liquid, gas, an
solid ice, and helps sha
Earth's surface.

The huge amounts of
on Earth help to expla
abundant life. Water i
important for life, bec
it allows chemicals
nutrients to move aro

EARTH PROFILE

Diameter: 12,742 km (7,918 miles)
Length of day: 23 h 56 m
Length of year: 365.25 days
Number of moons: One

During the water cycle, water vaporizes (becomes a gas) and rises to make clouds in our atmosphere.

Jigsaw Planet

Earth is made up of layers. At its core is a solid ball of iron and nickel, with an inner temperature of 5,400 °C (9,752 °F). Above this lies the mantle, made of molten rock, called magma. Earth's thin outer layer, or crust, is a jigsaw puzzle of giant pieces called plates that float on top of the magma. Over millions of years plates move apart or together, changing the shape and size of the continents and oceans.

Crust

Mantle

Plates move by a few cm (in) each year.

Outer core

Inner core

The Moon

Highland areas contain countless ancient craters.

Earth's constant partner, the Moon is the largest natural satellite compared to its planet in our solar system. It is an airless ball of rock covered in craters (bowl-shaped holes) formed when smaller objects smashed into it billions of years ago.

Seas and Highlands

The Moon's surface is a mix of dark, fairly smooth areas called seas or *maria*, and bright, cratered areas called highlands. The seas are what is left over of huge big craters that formed about four billion years ago. They were later flooded and then smoothed out by lava erupting from beneath the surface.

Lessons from *Apollo*

Twelve NASA astronauts walked on the surface of the Moon between 1969 and By studying its rocks and collecting samples they helped us understand the histo of the entire solar system—how the planets formed from countless smaller parti crashing together about 4.5 billion years ago. The Moon itself was created when Mars-sized planet slammed into Earth toward the end of this stage.

More recent craters spray debris (shards of rock) across the landscape.

Dark seas fill the outlines of large ancient craters.

The first manned Moon landing touched down in the Sea of Tranquility in July 1969.

This radar map shows high areas in yellow and red, and low areas in blue. It clearly shows a huge crater at the Moon's south pole.

Mars

The outermost rocky planet is also the one most like Earth. Mars today is a cold desert with thin, toxic air, but the newest discoveries have shown that it used to be much more welcoming, and that it might be again in the future.

Desert Planet?

Mars owes its famous red sands to large amounts of iron oxide, better known as rust. But sand dunes are only one part of the varied Martian landscape. Mars is also home to the largest volcano in the solar system (Olympus Mons, which is currently not active), and the deepest canyon, a huge crack in the surface called the Mariner Valley.

Martian Explorers

Mars is the best explored of all the other planets in the solar system. Many countries have sent space probes to map it from orbit, while NASA has landed wheeled rovers on the surface. Together, the different space agencies have shown that large amounts of water used to flow on Mars (it is now locked away as ice in the upper layers of soil). Is it possible there used to be life on this planet?

NASA's C
rover has
more than
(9 miles)
Martian s

MARS PROFILE

Diameter: 6,789 km (4,217 miles)
Length of day: 24 h 37 m
Length of year: 1.88 Earth years
Number of moons: Two

MARS

Two small, lumpy moons called Phobos (left) and Deimos orbit Mars. Astronomers are not sure if they formed alongside Mars, or used to be asteroids.

Bright ice caps at Mars's north and south poles are larger in winter and smaller in summer.

The northern half of the planet is mostly made up of smooth plains.

Air pressure on Mars is less than one percent of Earth's, and the atmosphere is mostly carbon dioxide.

Jupiter

Named after the ruler of the Roman gods, Jupiter is the largest planet in our solar system. This gas giant is the fifth planet, separated from the four inner, rocky planets by the asteroid belt. Ninety percent of Jupiter's atmosphere is hydrogen gas. Most of the rest is helium.

Red Spot Junior

Great Red Spot

Image by the Very Large Telescope

Image by *Hubble Space Telescope*

Little Red Spot

Red Spot Junior

Great Red Spot

The *Cassini* space probe took amazing photographs of Jupiter as it flew past in 2000 on its way to Saturn.

Two images of Jupiter's surface

Ganymede is the largest moon in the solar system.

Famous Feature

The most obvious feature on Jupiter's surface is the Great Red Spot—a massive storm that is more than twice Earth's diameter. It was first discovered in 1664 and has been raging ever since. Astronomers have found two other storms in the same cloud system, nicknamed Red Spot Junior and Little Red Spot.

Moons and Rings

Jupiter has more moons than any other planet in the solar

PLANET PROFILE

Diameter: 143,000 km (88,800 miles)
Length of day: 9 h 56 m
Length of year: 11.86 Earth years
Number of moons: 67

White bands of cloud are called zones.

Red–brown bands are called belts.

Saturn, Uranus and Neptune

The three giant planets of the outer solar system are all smaller than Jupiter. Saturn is quite similar to Jupiter, but Uranus and Neptune are "ice giants"—beneath their blue-green atmospheres they are mostly a mix of slushy chemicals including water.

Rings

Uranus has 13 rings
and 27 known moons.

World on its Side

Most of the solar system's
planets are a little tilted in their
orbits around the Sun, but only
Uranus is completely knocked
over on one side. This makes it
look like the planet "rolls" along
its orbit. It gives Uranus extreme
seasons—at the poles, winter is
one long night lasting almost 40
years, followed by a summer of
about the same length.

Uranus

Saturn's weather
bands are like
Jupiter's, but the
planet's clouds are
surrounded by a
creamy haze (fog).

Neptune

Storms on
Neptune look
like dark
spots. High
clouds seem
white.

Pluto and Beyond

Beyond the orbit of Neptune lies a ring of small frozen worlds called "ice dwarfs." Pluto, the most famous of these, was once called a planet in its own right. Even farther out is the Oort Cloud, a cloud of icy comets at the edge of the solar system.

Mysterious World

Pluto is a mix of rock and ice about half the size of the planet Mercury. Such a small, distant world was thought to be a deep-frozen ball of ice, but when NASA's *New Horizons* probe flew past in 2015, it showed a surprising world that may have been shaped by volcano-like eruptions of ice a long time ago.

Jan Oort discovered the the cloud that was later named after him by looking at the shapes and directions of comet orbits.

The temperature at the surface of Pluto ranges from –218 °C (–360 °F), when it is closest to the Sun, to –240 °C (–400 °F).

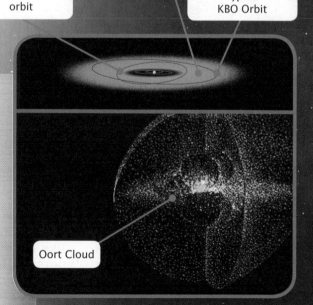

Kuiper Belt

Pluto's orbit

Typical KBO Orbit

Oort Cloud

Kuiper and Oort

The area where ice dwarfs orbit beyond Neptune is called the Kuiper Belt after astronomer Gerard Kuiper. He was one of the first people who thought there was such an area in our solar system. Objects that orbit here are often known as Kuiper Belt Objects (KBOs). From the edge of the Kuiper Belt, the huge Oort Cloud stretches out for almost a light-year, beginning as a broad disk, then opening out into a huge ball of icy, sleeping comets.

DWARF PLANET PROFILE

Diameter: 2,374 km (1,475 miles)
Length of day: 6.39 Earth days
Length of year: 248 Earth years
Number of moons: 5

Pluto's biggest moon, Charon, is more than half the size of Pluto itself.

Pluto's surface is mostly nitrogen, methane, and carbon monoxide ices.

Pluto might have active ice volcanoes even today.

Night and Day

Why is the sky dark at night and light in the daytime? It is all to do with how planet Earth is spinning in space. Half of the world faces toward the Sun at any one time, experiencing daytime, while the other half faces away and has night.

Daytime Skies

Why can't we see stars if we block out our view of the Sun? This is because Earth's atmosphere picks up and "scatters" sunlight from all parts of the sky. It glows a bright blue that drowns out even the brightest stars.

Look east (opposite the sunset) on a clear evening and see if you can spot the dark band of Earth's shadow rising up.

Time Zones

People have always used the movement of the Sun to keep time, but this means that "local time" is different wherever you are on Earth. Faster travel and communication in the 1800s led to the use of time zones. Each zone agrees on a standard time, rather than just using the Sun's position in the sky.

Greenwich Meridian (time is measured from here)

International Date Line (it is midnight here when it is noon on the Greenwich Meridian)

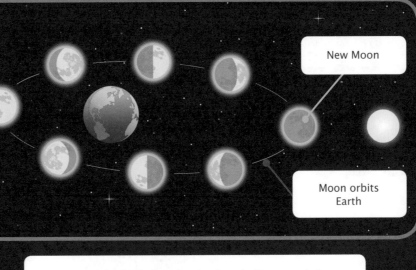

New Moon

Full Moon

Moon orbits Earth

During the 27.3 days that it takes the Moon to circle the Earth, we see different amounts of its sunlit face. This cycle is known as the phases of the Moon.

Close to Earth's north and south poles, the Sun never sets around midsummer—instead, it just dips close to the horizon around midnight before rising again.

Earth's Orbit

As Earth orbits the Sun once a year, it goes through a cycle of seasons. This is because the planet is tilted, so the northern and southern hemispheres (halves of Earth) get different amounts of sunlight at different times of year.

Tilted Earth

Earth's axis (an imaginary line that runs through the planet from pole to pole) is tipped at an angle of 23.5 degrees from upright, and points toward the pole star, Polaris. When the Sun also lies in this direction, it is summer in the northern hemisphere, with a high Sun and longer days, while the southern hemisphere has winter. Six months later, it is winter in the north and summer in the south.

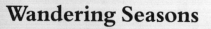

SUN

Wandering Seasons

Although Earth's axis points toward Polaris that isn't always the case. The direction of E wobbles in a 25,800 year cycle called precess cycle of seasons wanders with it. Scientists t makes a difference to Earth's climate, especi ages when the planet is colder than usual.

In summer, one hemisphere tilts toward the Sun. The Sun rises earlier, sets later, and crosses higher in the sky, warming the ground.

In autumn, Earth's axis once again points neither toward nor away from the Sun. Days become shorter and nights get longer.

In winter, one hemisphere tips away from the Sun. It rises later, sets earlier, and has a less warming effect because it crosses lower in the sky.

Astronomy

Seeing the wonders of space for yourself could not be easier. On a clear, dark night, anyone can stargaze. Special tools such as binoculars or telescopes can help you, but you can also see a lot with nothing more than your eyes.

Ready to Stargaze

To see as much as possible in the night sky, allow your eyes to get used to the dark. If you can, get out into the countryside, away from the glow of nearby cities. Be away from streetlights and phone screens, and do not shine flashlights. After about ten minutes you will find your eyes are much better at seeing faint stars.

Binoculars

How far can you see without a telescope? All the way to the Andromeda Galaxy, some 2.5 million light-years from Earth!

Many areas of the world are lit up at night. This makes it harder and harder to find really dark skies.

GALAXY PROFILE

Name: Andromeda galaxy
Catalogue number: Messier 31
Constellation: Andromeda
Distance from Earth: 2.5 million light-years
Description: This large spiral galaxy appears as a fuzzy blob of light in dark skies. Binoculars show its oval shape.

Telescopes

Telescopes are the most important tools astronom to look at objects in space. They gather up much light than our human eyes so that we can see fain objects, and they create a magnified (blown-up) image so that we can see much smaller details.

Two Designs

Telescopes come in two types. Refractors use two or more lenses at either end of a long tube to create a magnified image. Reflectors use a mirror to reflect light to a lens, and can have a more compact design. The job of the first lens or mirror is to collect light from a large area and bend or reflect it so that it passes through the smaller eyepiece lens.

Birth of the Telescope

The first telescopes were made by Dutch lensmakers around 1608, but the invention was made famous by Italian astronomer Galileo Galilei, who built his own telescope a few months later. He used it to make important discoveries, studying moons around Jupiter, craters on the Moon, and star clouds in the Milky Way.

TELESCOPE PROFILE

Name: Yerkes refractor
Built: 1897
Lens diameter: 102 cm (40 in)
Length: 19.2 m (63 ft)
Weight: 23.5 tonnes (26 tons)
Location: Williams Bay, Wisconsin, U.S.A.

A shutter opens to allow the telescope to see out into space.

An observatory dome protects the telescope from the weather.

A refracting telescope uses a big lens to bend light to a focus, and a smaller eyepiece to make a magnified image.

A stand holds the telescope's weight so that it can swivel with a gentle push.

A reflecting telescope uses two curved mirrors to collect and focus light, before passing it to a magnifying eyepiece.

Hubble Space Telescope

The most successful telescope ever built, the *Hubble Space Telescope* (*HST*) was the first large visible-light telescope ever put into space. From where it is above Earth's atmosphere, it has the clearest and sharpest views of the Universe.

HST has four bays for carrying many different cameras and other measuring instruments.

Radio antennae connect *HST* with its controllers on Earth using other satellites.

A special tube keeps the mirror safe from direct sunlight and extreme temperature changes.

Hubble has been repaired and upgraded by five space shuttle missions during its lifetime. The last was in 2009.

TELESCOPE PROFILE

Name: *Hubble Space Telescope*
Launch date: 1990
Mirror diameter: 2.4 m (7.9 ft)
Length: 13.2 m (43.5 ft)
Weight: 11,110 kg (24,500 lb)

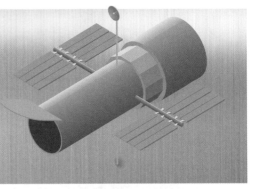

Clever Design

Sent into space in 1990, the *Hubble Space Telescope* is still working with up-to-date technology more than 25 years later. This is because it has a flexible design, with instrument units that can be replaced (removed, so that a newer unit can take its place) and upgraded. The telescope was named after the American astronomer Edwin Hubble.

An astronaut replaces one of *HST*'s instruments.

Solar panels make 1,200 watts of electricity to power the telescope and its instruments.

Discoveries

The *Hubble Space Telescope* has made many important discoveries. It has shown how stars are born in close-up for the first time, helped to discover some of the biggest stars and most distant galaxies in the Universe, and measured the speed at which our Universe is expanding (growing larger). Above all, it has taken amazing images that have forever changed the way we see space.

A *Hubble* image of the Arches, a giant star cluster near the middle of the Milky Way.

Rockets

Rising into space on a jet of flames, rockets need an explosive chemical reaction to push them through Earth's atmosphere. They are noisy, wasteful, and expensive, but they are still the best way of reaching orbit around the Earth.

Stage by Stage

Most rockets are made up of many "stages," each with their own fuel tanks and rocket engines. These stages may be stacked on top of each other, or sit side by side. Only the top stage reaches orbit with its cargo—the burnt-out lower stages fall back to Earth and are usually destroyed.

A ro
stage is
made
tanks
engines
small ca
the top
spa

Booster stages help to raise the speed of the top stage and cargo before falling back to Earth.

The *V–2* was a rocket with explosive cargo, used as a weapon during World War II. Most modern rockets are based on the *V–2*.

SPACECRAFT PROFILE

Name: *Saturn V*
Launch dates: 1967–73
Total launches: 13
Height: 110.6 m (363 ft)
Diameter: 10.1 m (33 ft)
Weight: 2.29 million kg (5.04 million lb)

Action and Reaction

Rockets rely on a rule that the English scientist Isaac Newton worked out in 1687: "For every action, there is an equal and opposite reaction." This means that the force of exploding gases coming from a rocket engine is always the same as the reaction: the force pushing the engine itself in the opposite direction. The rocket pushes against itself, not the air around it, so it can work even in space, where there is no air.

Isaac Newton discovered the principle of the rocket.

First stage with four rocket engines

Space Station

The *International Space Station* (ISS) is the ninth space station that humans have built in space. It is the first one where agencies from different countries have worked together—16 nations are part of the project. The *ISS* is the largest and most expensive spacecraft ever built.

Panel Power

The *ISS* has eight pairs of solar panels. Solar cells in the panels change energy from the Sun into electricity. A system of trusses (joining corridors) connects the different modules. They hold electrical lines, cooling lines for machines, and mobile transporter rails. The solar panels and robotic arms fix to the trusses, too.

Zvezda docking port

Solar panel

EACH SOLAR PANEL
MEASURES MORE
THAN THE WINGSPAN
OF A BOEING 777.

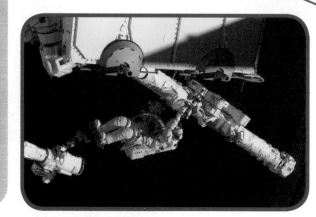

Life on the Station

The *ISS* has three laboratories: the Columbus laboratory, the Kibo laboratory and the U.S. Destiny laboratory. Every day, *ISS* crew carry out science experiments in the labs, and scientists on Earth also take part. There are research projects into making new materials and growing special crystals.

Kibo laboratory

U.S. Destiny laboratory

Columbus laboratory

Canadarm 2

NASA astronaut Karen Nyberg at work in the U.S. Destiny laboratory.

The first *ISS* module launched into orbit was the Russian–built Zarya, in 1998.

SPACECRAFT PROFILE

Name: *International Space Station*
Launch date: 1998 (latest module, 2017)
Width: 109 m (358 ft)
Length: 88 m (289 ft)
Weight: 419.6 tonnes (462.5 tons)
Orbiting speed: 8 km/s (17,895.5 mph)
Crew size: 3-6 people

Space

Humans have not made it farth[er]
Moon, but we have still been abl[e]
of the solar system using space p[robes]
explorers have now visited all th[e]
and many smaller worlds, too.

Specialist Robots

Probes are designed to carry out one
kind of mission. Some probes
are orbiters that will become
satellites of other planets.
Others may carry out high-
speed flyby missons and

Cameras are fixed to a long arm.

Full Speed to Pluto

Most probes take many years to reach those planets that are farther away, but in 2006 NASA launched a high-speed mission that planned to reach Pluto in just nine years. *New Horizons* became the fastest spacecraft ever launched when it left Earth at 56,000 km/h (36,000 mph). It picked up even more speed along the way thanks to a "slingshot" around the giant planet Jupiter.

Electricity is generated (made) by a tiny amount of radioactive fuel.

A large radio dish sends and receives signals to and from the distant Earth.

New Horizons reached Pluto on 14 July 2015. The information it collected in a few hours took 16 months to send back to Earth.

Big Ban

Our Universe was born 13.8 billion (thou
a huge explosion called the Big Bang. Th
all the matter in the Universe, but also sp
meaningless to ask where it happened, o

Discovery

The Russian scientist Alexander
Friedmann was the first person to suggest
that the Universe might be expanding
(growing), in 1924. The American Edwin
Hubble proved this in 1929. The Belgian
Georges Lemaître followed the expansion
backward and stated that the Universe
began in a hot, dense ball of matter.

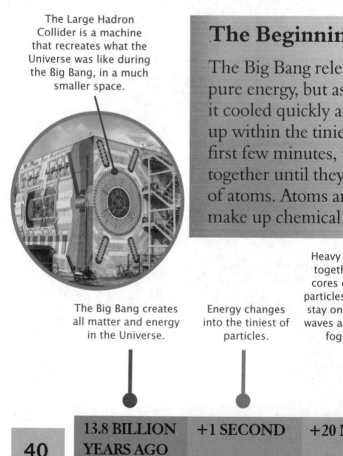

The Large Hadron
Collider is a machine
that recreates what the
Universe was like during
the Big Bang, in a much
smaller space.

The Beginnin

The Big Bang rele
pure energy, but as
it cooled quickly a
up within the tinie
first few minutes,
together until they
of atoms. Atoms ar
make up chemical

Heavy
togeth
cores
particles
stay on
waves a
fog

The Big Bang creates
all matter and energy
in the Universe.

Energy changes
into the tiniest of
particles.

13.8 BILLION
YEARS AGO

+1 SECOND

+20 l

Galaxies and stars formed about 150 million years after the Big Bang itself.

The Universe is a huge expanding bubble, but there is no way of getting outside it.

During the Big Bang, energy could change into mass and back, creating the building blocks of matter.

Galaxies

Galaxies are groups of stars, gas, and dust. Some are huge balls of trillions of stars and others are small clouds of just a few million. Pulled together by the force of gravity, these clouds become factories for making new stars.

Crowded Universe

Galaxies are huge objects—tens or even hundreds of thousands of light-years across, and with powerful gravity that have an effect on the galaxies nearest to them. This means that they tend to crowd together in some places, forming clusters of anything from tens to thousands of galaxies. On the largest scales, clusters join together to form superclusters that are hundreds of millions of light-years wide.

This "Hubble Deep Field" holds 5,500 galaxies.

Galaxy Types

Astronomers group galaxies into many different kinds. The most important are spirals (disks with spiral arms where the brightest stars are close together) and ellipticals (balls of red and yellow stars that look like the cores of spirals). There are also irregulars (shapeless clouds, often made up of many bright stars).

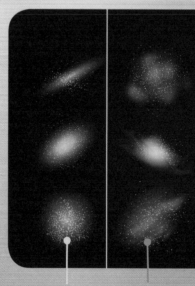

Elliptical galaxies

Irregular galaxies

Spiral galaxies

The oldest galaxies in this image look like they did 13.2 billion years ago.

This image was created when the *Hubble Space Telescope* focused on what looked like an empty area of space for 23 days.

The most distant galaxies are shapeless blobs. They are still being formed.

Stars

Stars are born in huge clouds of gas and dust called nebulae. They begin their lives as collapsing knots of gas that grow hotter and denser for perhaps a million years, until conditions at the core are able to turn hydrogen into helium.

Infrared shines through the dust to show glowing gas, warmed by newborn stars.

An infrared view of part of the Horsehead Nebula region of Orion.

Brought into Being

Star-birth nebulae are some of the most beautiful sights in the Universe. As the stars inside begin to shine, they make the gas nearby glow. Different elements create

STAR-FORMING NEBULAE

Carina

This nebula is the largest and brightest in the sky, but is only visible in southern skies.

Eagle

Stars are born inside these towers of gas and dust in the constellation Serpens, the Snake.

Horsehead

Seen as a whole, the famous Horsehead Nebula in Orion looks like a chesspiece.

The Horsehead is just one part of a much larger star factory.

Planet Hunting

Astronomers use two main methods to look for planets. One way is to look for the tiny wobbles in a star's movement that are caused by an orbiting planet pulling it in different directions. Another is to watch for tiny dips in a star's brightness that happen when a planet is passing in front of it. With both methods it is easier to find giant planets, similar to Jupiter, rather than smaller ones.

Planet hunters have found a lot of "hot Jupiters"—giant exoplanets orbiting very near their stars.

This image of a planetary system called HR8799 was taken by the Keck Observatory.

NEBULA PROFILE

Name: Orion Nebula
Catalogue number: Messier 42
Distance: 1,340 light-years
Constellation: Orion
Size: Approx 25 light-years wide
Description: The heart of a huge star-forming region that spreads across Orion.

Glossary

ASTRONOMICAL UNIT
Earth's distance from the Sun—about 150 million km (93 million miles).

ATMOSPHERE
A shell of gases kept around a planet, star, or other object by its gravity.

EXOPLANET
A planet orbiting a star outside our solar system.

GALAXY
A large system of stars, gas, and dust with anything from millions to trillions of stars.

GIANT PLANET
A planet much larger than Earth, made up of gas, liquid, and slushy frozen chemicals.

GRAVITY
A natural force created around objects with mass, which draws other objects toward them.

KUIPER BELT
A ring of small icy worlds directly beyond the orbit of Neptune. Pluto is the largest known Kuiper Belt Object.

LIGHT-YEAR
The distance light travels in a year—about 9.5 trillion km (5.9 trillion miles).

MOON
Earth's closest companion in space, a ball of rock that orbits Earth every 27.3 days. Most other planets in the solar system have moons of their own.

NEBULA
A cloud of gas or dust floating in space. Nebulae are the raw material used to make stars.

ORBIT
A fixed path taken by one object in space around another because of the effect of gravity.

PLANET
A world that orbits the Sun, which has enough mass and gravity to pull itself into a ball-like shape, and clear space around it of other large objects.

ROCKET
A vehicle that drives itself forward through a controlled chemical explosion and can therefore travel in the vacuum of space. Rockets are the only practical way to launch spacecraft and satellites.

ROCKY PLANET
An Earth-sized or smaller planet, made up mostly of rocks and minerals, sometimes with a thin outer layer of gas and water.

SATELLITE
Any object orbiting a planet. Moons are natural satellites made of rock and ice. Artificial (human-made) satellites are machines in orbit around Earth.

SPACE PROBE
A robot vehicle that explores the solar system and sends back signals to Earth.

SPACECRAFT
A vehicle that travels into space.

SPIRAL GALAXY
A galaxy with a hub of old yellow stars (sometimes crossed by a bar) surrounded by a flattened disk of younger stars, gas, and dust. Bright newborn stars make a spiral pattern across the disk.

TELESCOPE
A device that collects light or other radiations from space and uses them to create a bright, clear image. Telescopes can use either a lens or a mirror to collect light.